MW00929420

Top Ten Facts About Eclipses

ROBERTA BAXTER

Copyright © 2017 Roberta Baxter

All rights reserved.

ISBN-10: 1548803243
ISBN-13: 978-1548803247

DEDICATION

To all who gaze into the skies and wonder.

CONTENTS

INTRODUCTION

We gaze in wonder at the multitude of stars, the planets as they orbit our sun, the sun and the moon. But one of the most spectacular sights is an eclipse. It's fun to see a lunar eclipse or a solar eclipse. Everyone should take a chance to see these fascinating events.

The author experienced a total eclipse in February, 1979, while living in North Dakota. The sky darkened quickly and there was quiet up and down our street even though many people were standing in their driveways, safely viewing the event. The already cold temperature dropped even more. The shadows on the snowbanks next to the driveways seemed strange because they were not in the usual place. Seeing the moon cross in front of the sun, starting with a bite out of the sun and then completely covering it, was an inspiring sight that sent shivers down the back.

Then before we got used to the darkness, the sun began to emerge from behind the moon, the temperature rose slightly, and everyone up and down the street cheered.

This book covers ten facts about eclipses. It will answer questions you might have about how eclipses happen, how often they happen, and how you can safely view one.

FACT 1
HOW DOES A SOLAR ECLIPSE HAPPEN?

We use the word, eclipse, for events in the sky. But the word eclipse means one object moves in front of another object. If a person wearing a big hat blocks your view of a movie screen, the movie screen is eclipsed by that person and their hat.

In astronomy, the study of the universe, an eclipse happens when one space body moves in front of another. A solar eclipse occurs when the Earth, the moon and the sun line up. The moon passes between Earth and the sun. The moon covers the face of the sun. The moon is much smaller than the Earth or the sun. But it is closer to Earth than the sun. When it is in between us and the sun, the sun is covered.

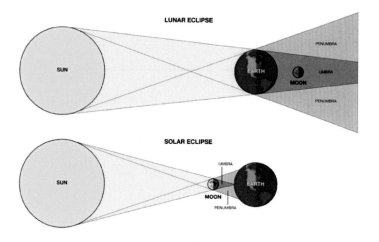

You can picture this with three balls. Imagine that a basketball is the sun. Put it away from you as far as you can in your backyard. Now hold a ping pong ball in front of you as far as you can reach out your arm. Line up the two balls. The ping pong ball can cover the basketball even though it is smaller. This is because the ping pong ball is much closer to you than the basketball.

When a solar eclipse happens, we see the dark shape of the shadow of the moon in front of the sun. Only the edge of the sun is still shining. Darkness falls on the Earth in a narrow band. Outside of that band, observers will see part of the sun covered by the moon, but not the whole sun. As the Earth turns, the shadow of the moon moves across the face of the Earth. During the darkness of a total eclipse, stars and planets will shine out brightly.

Solar eclipses are rare. The Earth orbits the sun and the moon orbits the Earth. The orbits are not circles. The shapes are called ellipses. They are longer in one direction than the other. The moon takes close to a month to orbit the Earth and Earth takes a year to orbit the sun.

The moon also orbits the Earth at a tilted angle from the Earth's orbit around the sun. An eclipse can only happen at the node points.

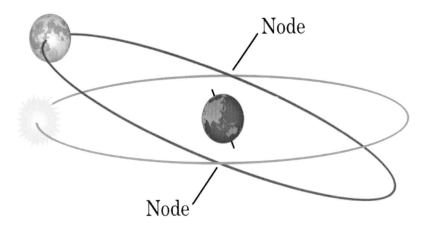

The elliptical orbits and the tilt of the moon's orbit mean that the Earth, moon and sun do not line up very often and cause an eclipse.

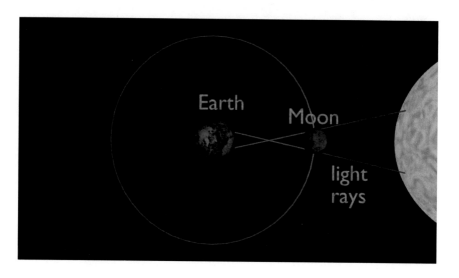

FACT 2
HOW DOES A LUNAR
ECLIPSE HAPPEN?

A lunar eclipse comes when the Earth moves between the sun and the moon. The moon does not shine with its own light. It reflects light from the sun. The moon has a different look to us on Earth through a month.

The moon always points the same face toward the Earth. It is locked in that position. As the moon orbits the Earth, we see different angles of the moon. First it is a bright round disk in the sky. That is the full moon. We see the entire side of the moon that it lit up by the sun. Then it becomes a half moon. We see only part of the shiny side of the moon. Then a tiny sliver of a moon is in the sky, showing only a small part of the lit side of the moon. Next is the new moon, when all we see is a dark moon that shows none of its shiny side. The side of the moon that is reflecting the sun's rays is turned away from the Earth. Then the sliver and the half moon come back. The moon goes through this cycle every 29.5 days.

A lunar eclipse can only happen at full moon. The shiny face of the moon is seen from Earth. The Earth moves between the moon and the sun. The light of the sun cannot hit the moon because the Earth is in the way. The shadow of the Earth moves across the moon, so at the start of the eclipse, it looks like a big bite has been taken out of the moon. Eventually, the shadow of the Earth will cover the moon. Then it will start to move away from the moon.

If you see a lunar eclipse, the moon might look red. This happens because of the atmosphere that surrounds the Earth. Some of the light from the sun goes through the atmosphere and is bent, much like the formation of a rainbow. The other colors of the spectrum are scattered by the Earth's atmosphere, but the red makes it through so we can see it.

When a lunar eclipse happens, everyone on the night side of Earth can see it. You are more likely to see several lunar eclipses in your lifetime, but only one or two solar eclipses.

The progress of a lunar eclipse

FACT 3
WHAT KIND OF SOLAR
ECLIPSES HAPPEN?

Not all solar eclipses are the same. You might see three kinds of solar eclipses—partial, annular, and total.

A partial eclipse happens when only part of the sun is covered by the moon. From Earth, it looks like a bite has been taken out of the sun. The moon never completely covers the sun. Soon the bite shrinks and then the sun is back to full shine.

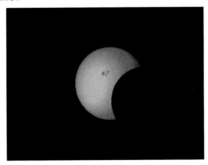

Partial Eclipse

An annular eclipse occurs when the moon is further from the Earth. Because the moon is further away, it appears smaller than usual. Remember, the orbit of the moon around the Earth is an ellipse, not a circle. When the moon is further away and moves in front of the sun, we still see an eclipse. But a bright rim of the sun still shows around the edges.

Annular Eclipse

When the moon completely covers the sun, it is a total eclipse. The moon is closer to the Earth, so the moon seems larger. It will fit over the whole face of the sun. Only the corona of the sun will be seen around the moon. The word, corona, comes from a word for crown. It means the outer atmosphere of the sun, seen as a shining ring around the moon.

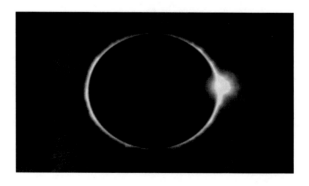

Total Eclipse

During a total eclipse, some people will be outside the darkest part of the moon's shadow. They will see a partial eclipse of the sun. In the diagram, you can see that only a small section of the ground will see a total eclipse. This is in the deepest shadow, called the umbra. Around the umbra is a section of shadow, but not as strong as the center. This is called the penumbra. If you are in the area of the penumbra, you see a partial eclipse.

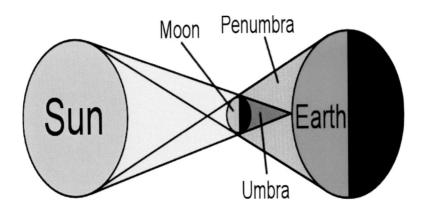

FACT 4
HOW OFTEN DO ECLIPSES HAPPEN?

Solar eclipses happen about every 18 months. They occur in different places on Earth and many times they are partial or annular eclipses, not total.

Total eclipses at a specific point may be hundreds of years apart. For example, if you live in Denver, Colorado, the last total eclipse was in 1878. The next total one won't be until 2045. These two are 167 years apart. For Los Angeles, California, the time between total solar eclipses is more than 1500 years.

This difference in times happens because the orbits of the Earth and moon are not circles. Scientists have to use advanced math to figure out when the next eclipse will be.

Total solar eclipses are seen in a narrow path across the Earth with a larger strip that sees a partial eclipse. Lunar eclipses can be seen by everyone on the night side of Earth.

More people see lunar eclipses than solar. Any spot on Earth will see a lunar eclipse about every 2.5 years.

Lucky people living in the town of Carbondale, Illinois will get to see two total solar eclipses in seven years. The first will be August 21, 2017 and the next will be in 2024.

FACT 5
WHAT HAPPENS TO
ANIMALS
DURING A SOLAR ECLIPSE?

People have observed that animals, birds and insects sometimes change their behavior during a solar eclipse.

Scientists watched a group of chimpanzees in a Primate Research Center. The chimps showed that they knew something was going on during a solar eclipse. The eclipse happened in the middle of the day. As the sky darkened, the females with infants moved to the top of a climbing structure. Then the rest of the chimpanzees joined them and turned their bodies toward the sun. Once the sun began to reappear, the chimpanzees returned to their normal activity.

Another study showed that horses and cattle became quiet and sniffed the air. They knew something was not right. They were restless, swishing their tails and shaking their heads.

Squirrels seem to run more during an eclipse. They sense the strange light levels and become more active. Maybe they are trying to run away from the darkness.

Birds are affected even more than animals. As the sun disappears, wild birds and chickens think it is night. They go back to their nests and become silent. People who see an eclipse say that it becomes very quiet because birds stop singing and flying. Once the sun is shining again, they fly, cluck and sing as usual. Night flying birds, such as owls, begin waking up and moving around in the darkness. They return to sleep as the sun brightens.

Insects are also affected by the lack of sunlight. Bees are more restless and move in and out of the hives more than usual. Cicadas in the deserts of southwestern United States were singing as normal in the early morning of an eclipse in 1991. When the sun was 50% covered, they stopped their calls. Researchers thought this might be a result of the temperature being cooler than when the sun was out.

If you ever experience a total solar eclipse, maybe you can see how your pets and animals around you react. Pets may not act differently because they are used to lights inside our homes.

FACT 6
WHAT WOULD A LUNAR ECLIPSE
LOOK LIKE FROM THE MOON?

A lunar eclipse happens when the Earth comes between the moon and the sun. If you are on the moon, the Earth is between you and the sun. The Earth eclipses the sun.

When the Earth moves between the sun and a person on the moon, you would see a reddish light around you because the sun's rays are being bent by the Earth's atmosphere. The same thing happens in a lunar eclipse seen from Earth. As the shadow of the Earth covers the moon, the surface would be in deep darkness. Then the shadow would move and the reddish light would reappear.

One of the most interesting things in seeing a lunar eclipse from the moon is what happens to the Earth. The sun is behind the Earth. Its rays and light make a fiery ring around the Earth.

Some American astronauts saw the Earth eclipse the sun. As Alan Bean, Pete Conrad and Dick Gordon returned from landing on the moon with Apollo 12, they saw the Earth move in front of the sun. Alan Bean wrote, "We were seeing our home planet Earth eclipse our own star, the Sun. …the Earth moved to completely obscure the disk of the sun." The Earth was dark with the ring of fire from the sun encircling it. They also saw a mysterious round bright circle showing on the darkness of the Earth. Later they learned that circle was the reflection of the bright full moon shining behind their spacecraft.

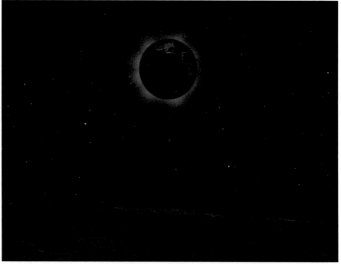

Drawing of what a lunar eclipse would look like from the moon by NASA's Scientific Visualization Studio

FACT 7
ARE THERE ECLIPSES
ON OTHER PLANETS?

Other planets in our solar system have moons. Sometimes those moons are eclipsed by their planets. Jupiter and Saturn are so large that when they block the rays of the sun, their moons experience a long eclipse.

The Cassini spacecraft is orbiting Saturn. In 2006, its cameras captured Saturn moving in front of the sun, throwing the spacecraft into the dark shadow. During this event, the cameras showed the rings of Saturn as never before and scientists learned a lot more about the rings.

Photo from the Cassini spacecraft:

photojournal.jpl.nasa.gov

Two planets in our solar system—Mercury and Venus—do not have moons, so they do not experience eclipses.

Mars has two moons. In 2012, the Curiosity Rover, on the surface of Mars, took a video of one of the moons, Phobos, eclipsing the sun. Phobos is small enough that it can't completely cover the sun, so it only covers part of the sun. You can see the video at:
https://youtu.be/OyZoD7BRTtg?t=78

FACT 8
WHAT ABOUT ECLIPSES
IN HISTORY?

Ancient people were terrified when they saw an eclipse. They knew how the moon and sun were supposed to look and move. They understood that they depended on the sun for warmth and life. Imagine how you would feel if some giant beast took a bite out of the sun.

Historical records show that the ancient Babylonians and Chinese had figured out how to predict eclipses 4500 years ago. In China, it was thought that failing to predict an eclipse caused the emperor to be in danger. Two men did not predict an eclipse in 2134 and they were killed for it. Babylonian clay tablets show that they correctly predicted an eclipse in 1375 BCE.

A Greek historian writes that a solar eclipse in 585 BCE convinced two countries at war to make peace. They saw the dark sky as a sign that the gods were not happy with their fighting.

Pueblo people lived in the American Southwest over 1,000 years ago. Some of what we know about them is from pictures they drew on rocks. One shows a circle, representing the sun, surrounded by wispy strands, much like the corona. Nearby is a dot that would be exactly where the planet Venus was during an eclipse seen by the Puebloans in 1097.

Pictograph from Chaco Canyon

Native Americans from the area of northern California had a story explaining a solar eclipse. They said that a bear walks along the Milky Way. When the sun refuses to move out of his way, the bear takes a bite. Next, he fights the sun's sister, the moon, and she refuses to move. A great fight occurs in the sky and eventually the sun and moon are victorious and return to their normal shape.

Christopher Columbus is known for discovering the New World. He made four voyages across the Atlantic

Ocean. On his fourth voyage, he almost lost his life. Two of his ships had to be abandoned because of worms that ate holes in the wood. He landed the other two and his crews in Jamaica on June 25, 1503. At first, the natives welcomed them. But after six months, the Jamaicans were tired of feeding them. Columbus' crews were rebelling and some men committed crimes against the Jamaicans. It looked like they would be fighting a war.

But Columbus had a book that showed that a lunar eclipse was approaching on February 29, 1504. He told the chief that his god was angry with the Jamaicans and he would prove it. In three nights, the god would cause the moon to show his anger. When the moon seemed to be disappearing and the red color was displayed, the natives were terrified. Columbus then told them that the god was pleased with their response and so the moon would return to normal.

After that demonstration, the natives continued to help Columbus and his men until help arrived from Spain. Columbus and his men left Jamaica.

Moon during a lunar eclipse

Watch for more books in the "Top Ten Facts About" series. Coming soon!

FACT 9
WHEN ARE THE NEXT ECLIPSES?

The next total solar eclipse happens on August 21, 2017. It has been called The Great American Eclipse because it will cross the continental United States and not any other country.

The eclipse will darken a strip of land about 70 miles wide from Oregon to South Carolina. Outside of that narrow line will be a stretch of partial eclipse. The eclipse will move across the country from west to east. It will start at 10:15 a.m. Pacific Daylight Time and leave the country at 2:45 p.m. Eastern Daylight Time. In each place, the total eclipse will last a little more than 2 minutes.

People around the country are planning eclipse watch parties. Many public libraries have special displays and events planned for the eclipse.

The next total solar eclipse that will be seen in the

United States is April 8, 2024. There is a total eclipse that will be seen in parts of South America on July 2, 2019.

Remember that lunar eclipses occur more often and are seen by more people. There will be one on January 31, 2018 that will be seen by Northern and Eastern Europe, Asia, Australia, Northern and Eastern Africa, North America, Northern and Western South America, the Pacific Ocean, the Atlantic Ocean, the Indian Ocean, the Artic and Antarctica.

FACT 10
HOW CAN I SAFELY
VIEW A SOLAR ECLIPSE?

You know that you should NEVER look at the sun. It takes only seconds for your eyes to be damaged by looking at the sun. So how can you safely observe a solar eclipse?

In years past, people would use smoked glass to view an eclipse. That is not safe because the smoke does not block out enough of the dangerous rays. Sunglasses are also not protective enough. Don't look through the viewfinder of a camera to take a photo of the eclipse.

You can buy solar eclipse glasses. Four companies have been certified as having safe ones: Rainbow Symphony, American Paper Optics, Thousand Oaks Optical, and TSE 17. You can also find solar eclipse viewing glasses on Amazon.

One safe way to observe a solar eclipse involves not looking at the sun at all. You can make a pinhole projector from items you have at home. You will need two pieces of cardboard. Make a tiny pinhole in the center of one piece of cardboard. Then, with your back to the sun, let the light fall through the hole and onto the other piece of cardboard held at arm's length. You will be able to see an image of the sun as the moon takes the bite out and as it covers the sun. To make an even sharper pinhole and a sharper image, cut a rectangle out of the top piece of cardboard. Tape a piece of aluminum foil over that hole and prick a small pinhole through the foil. Then line the pieces of cardboard up as before. The image of the sun will be small, but clear. The further you can put the pieces of cardboard apart (by having someone else hold one), the bigger the image will be.

Enjoy any eclipse that you have a chance to see, whether the one coming in August 2017 or later ones. Both solar and lunar eclipses are a joy to witness.

RESOURCES

NASA eclipse web site:
https://www.nasa.gov/audience/forstudents/5-8/features/nasa-knows/what-is-an-eclipse-58

Mr. Eclipse Site:
http://www.mreclipse.com/Special/SEprimer.html

Eclipse glasses
Rainbow Symphony eclipse glasses:
http://www.eclipseglasses2017.com/

American Paper Optics: https://www.eclipseglasses.com/

Thousand Oaks Optical:
http://thousandoaksoptical.com/products/eclipse/

TSE17: http://tse17.com/eclipse-shop/

Make a Pinhole Projector
https://www.exploratorium.edu/eclipse/how-to-view-eclipse

ABOUT THE AUTHOR

Roberta Baxter writes about science and history for students of all ages. She is looking forward to the next eclipses.

46867049R00022

Made in the USA
Middletown, DE
11 August 2017